What's for lunch

Banana

Pam Robson

W
FRANKLIN WATTS
LONDON•SYDNEY

What's for lunch?

Banana

This edition 2003

Franklin Watts
96 Leonard Street
London
EC2A 4XD

Franklin Watts Australia
45-51 Huntley Street
Alexandria
NSW 2015

Editor: Samantha Armstrong
Series Designer: Kirstie Billingham
Designer: Dalia Hartman
Consultant: Paul Barrett
Reading Consultant: Prue Goodwin, Reading and Language
Information Centre, Reading

A CIP catalogue record for this book is available from the British Library
Dewey Decimal Classification Number 641.3

ISBN: 0 7496 4944 5

Printed in Hong Kong, China

Today we are having a banana for lunch.
We eat bananas as a **fruit**,
but they are also used to flavour lots of foods.
Bananas contain **vitamins**, **proteins** and **fibre**.
Eating bananas will give you **energy**.

Bananas grow on plants.
The plants look like trees but,
instead of a trunk, they have
a stem made from leaf stalks
rolled around each other.
One leaf can be big enough
to use as an umbrella!

Bananas grow in countries
where it is always hot
and where, for part of the year,
there is also a lot of rain.
Farmers in the West Indies
grow bananas.
Their bananas are sometimes
destroyed by strong winds
called **hurricanes**.
The farmers grow their bananas
among tall trees to protect
them from the wind.

Some of the bananas we buy
are grown on large farms
called **plantations**.

In the past **rainforest** was cut down to make room for the plantations. Many people thought this was wrong because it destroyed wildlife.

Some fruits like apples have **seeds** called pips inside them. When the pips are planted, new apple trees grow.

Bananas do not grow from seeds. Instead a **sucker** grows from the plant **root.** The sucker will become a new banana plant. The farmers put the new plant into the earth.

13

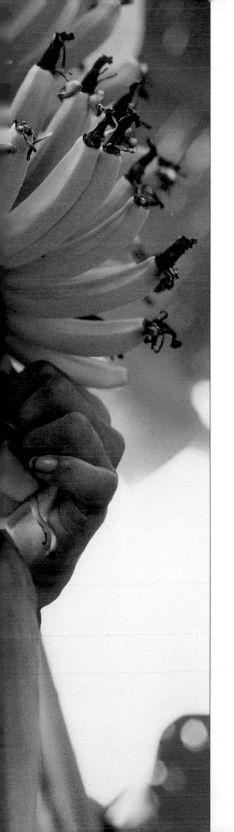

The farmers are always busy
looking after the growing plants.
They trim them so that
the bananas will have
room to grow.
They also check to make sure
there are no pests or diseases
on the plants.

Each plant grows one **stem**
with up to 200 bananas on it.
A large bunch of bananas is called
a **hand,** and each banana
is called a **finger.**
The bananas bend upwards
towards the sun
and become curved.

The farmers cover the bananas
with special **sleeves**
to protect them from pests
and bad weather.

After a year, the bananas
are ready to be picked.
They are still green.
Each stem is cut off the plant
with a knife called a **machete**.
It takes two people to do this
as the stem is very heavy.
The bananas are hung from
moving cables that take them to
the packing station.

In the packing station the bananas are washed in large baths of cold water. The water also keeps the bananas cool. Bananas are easily damaged so they are packed quickly and carefully into boxes.

The boxes of bananas are taken to
special ships that have cool compartments.

These keep the fruit fresh
on its long journey.

On arrival some bananas
are placed in special ripening centres.
There they are warmed until they ripen.
This means that they are still fresh
when we buy them.
Bananas are used
to flavour lots of things,
like milkshakes and yoghurt.

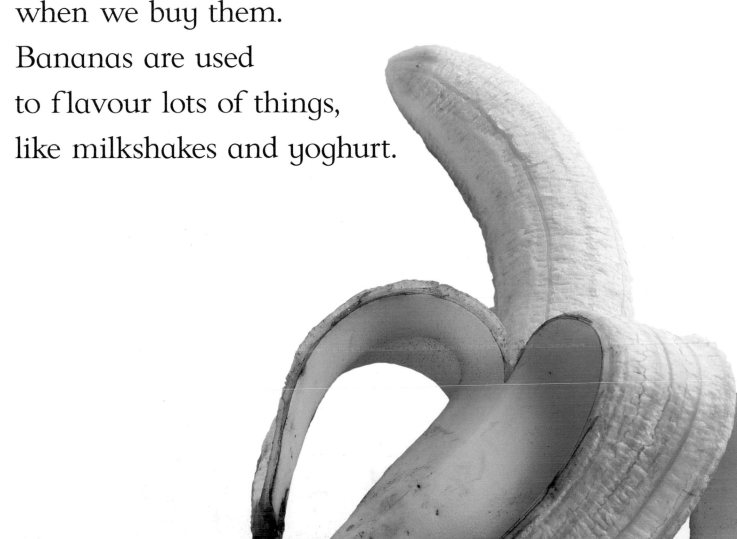

Bananas can be cooked.
They can be made into a banoffi pie
or a banana cake.
Sometimes bananas are dried
so that they last longer.
They can be eaten as a snack
or in breakfast cereal.

Some fresh fruits, like raspberries,
can only be found in our shops
at certain times of the year.
But bananas are always there.
They are delicious.

Glossary

energy   the strength to work and play

fibre   something found in some foods
that helps you to digest what you eat

finger   a single banana growing in a bunch

fruit   a food that usually grows on a tree or a bush
such as apple, orange or banana

hand   a bunch of bananas

hurricane   a storm with very strong winds

machete   a heavy knife with a wide blade which is
used to cut the thick banana stems

plantation   a large area of land which is used to grow one
kind of plant such as coffee, tea or bananas

protein   something found in foods like milk, cheese,
bananas and meat that helps to build the
body and keep it healthy

rainforest	thick forest found in the hot, rainy parts of the world. Many different animals and plants live there
root	the part of a plant that grows downwards into the soil and takes in goodness and water to help the plant to grow
seed	the part of a plant which grows into a new plant
sleeve	a plastic covering with open ends that farmers put over the bananas to protect them against cold weather or rain
stem	the part of a plant that supports the leaf, fruit and flower
sucker	a new shoot growing from the root of a banana plant
vitamin	something that is found in fresh fruit and vegetables that keeps the body healthy

Index

Picture credits: Bruce Coleman 7 (Peter Terry); Courtesy of Fyffes 13, 14, 20; NHPA 15 (Stephen Dalton); Panos Pictures 10-11 (Neil Cooper), 16 (Philip Wolmuth), 19 (Paul Smith), 22-3 (Paul Smith), 24-5 (Philip Wolmuth) Robert Harding 8 (G. Corrigan); Nick Bailey Photography cover, 3, 5. All other photographs Tim Ridley, Wells Street Studios, London. **With thanks to Ushil Patel and Edward Evans.**